A Walking Cliché Coins a Phrase

A Walking Cliché Coins a Phrase

Prose Poems, Letters and Microfictions

Chad Prevost

Plain View Press
P. O. 42255
Austin, TX 78704

plainviewpress.net
sb@plainviewpress.net
1-512-441-2452

Copyright Chad Prevost 2008. All rights reserved.
ISBN: 978-1-891386-37-4
Library of Congress Number: 2008937237

Cover art by Clayton Anderson

Acknowledgements

Thanks to the following where nearly all of these were previously published:

Magazines: *Asheville Poetry Review, Askew, The Chattahoochee Review, Cimarron Review, Main Street Rag, New South, Nightsun, Pearl, Pinyon Poetry, Poem, Poemeleon (zine), Poetry Superhighway (zine), The Potomac (zine), Re:al, Redactions, Red River Review (zine), Salt Hill, The Seattle Review, Sentence, The Southeast Review, Tattoo Highway (zine)*

Anthologies: *Bear Flag Republic: California Prose Poems and Poetics* (Alcatraz Editions), *Blackbox Recorder* (Las Vegas)

Chapbook: Several of these were published for the first time in *Chasing the Gods* by Pudding House Press: "Where the Light is Still Good," "Break Up Letter under the Influence," "Chad Prevost Chases Chad Prevost to Make Sure the Future Comes True."

Eliah and Lucas

Contents

Acknowledgements   5

1   Seven Lightning Strikes

Fever	13
The Meaning of Chad	14
The Aging Rock Star	15
Screenplay Plot for *A Walking Cliché Coins a Phrase*	16
Day in the Life	18
Notes from Jesus	19
Seven Lightning Strikes	20

2   The End of the World

The End of the World	25
Three Rose Tattoo	26
Rehearsing	27
Muted Blues Bird	28
Letter to Plant from Easter Island	29
Letter to (Un)Resurrected Messiah	30
Where Prevost was Conceived	31
Poem Escaping through Holes in the Ozone	33

3   The Book of Masters

Dear Order and Meaning,	37
Dear Narrowing Gyre,	38
Letter to Zarathustra from Hypochondriac	39
Letter to Jordan from an Economy-Sized Best Western	40
Letter to Bonds from Savings and Loan	41
Letter to a Suicide Letter	42
Break-Up Letter under the Influence	43
Dear I Am Already a Mountain Range,	44
Dear Light Those at Work See,	45
Letter from Branch Manager of Terminal Accounts ...	46

4   What Volcanologists Know

Notes Toward What Volcanologists Know	49
On the Identity Formation of Prevost	50
Bowing Not Knowing to What	52
A Walking Cliché Tries Not to Peek at the Cleavage ...	53
Dear Life-size Muse,	54
Chad Prevost Chases Chad Prevost to Make Sure ...	55
The Dead Among Us	57
Baptism by Fire	58

5   Insomniac

Where the Light is Still Good	61
What is Today?	62
Redeemed	63
Following My Calling	64
Tantrum	65
No Home	66
Dear Just Visiting this Planet,	67
Signs as Clues and Sometimes Wonders	68
If You Want to Be Famous	69
Insomniac	70

Notes	71
About the Author	73

1 Seven Lightning Strikes

Fever

Am I in the right bed, the one with an imprint of my body shaped like a fossil into the life I bartered for as Professor, Husband, Father, uncapitalized Capitalist, a man with a neatly trimmed yard? Or is my dream whirl-pooling away like the tug boats in my son's bath? Am I in my right mind, the one I left at the dinner table? Or am I pushing away from the shore of another life? Am I asking to be excused before I finish my peas? My father has come to take me back. He who immersed me in the Baptistery by the Bay at Tiburon Baptist—*El tiburon*, the name for shark—has freed me from my recovery. No longer must I wear a gown of shame, or sit in a Time Out cell, or profess in the 12 Steps. The counselors have given me back the items they took from my person—razor blades, acne medication, bracelets, marijuana, pipe, Zippo. Is it true? Have we sailed around the world from Sausalito to Deltaville, from San Pablo to the Chesapeake? Are we in his *Catalina 25*? Or are we a vessel from the Old World, armed with a mission, ready to sail off the world's edge to bring Good News? It's early Fall, maybe October. The light is a resinous orange, which could be turning the world to dawn or dusk. In the visible depths, the bay is a universe filled with jellyfish the size of baby fists. We're tacking into the headwind, the choppy spray, the fog, the barely visible world.

The Meaning of Chad

Every day it seems chad stands for something else. Some say chad is related to *chit* and *chaff*, meaning *small residue*. Chad's usage has plummeted ever since the Campaign of 2000 in which chad was referred to as dimpled, hanging, swinging, and pregnant. Attorneys have made it clear that pregnancy does not count in Palm Beach County, only penetration. Chad's reputation has never been the same. It doesn't help that even as we speak Chaddian rebels have broken through Chad's eastern defenses. Groups have been fighting over The Republic of Chad for at least 2500 years. Chad may be one of the poorest countries in the world, but Chad prefers not to be thought of as *small residue*. It's true, Chad's median age remains stuck at 16, and inside Chad 200 distinct ethnic groups survive. Still, some pockets inside remain hopeful. Chad yearns to be a better place, located as Chad is, in an ancient cradle of civilization. Chad wants to prove Chad's real character not by resiliency in the face of disease and hunger, but in the parts of Chad that have all the power and the way that power is used. Chad's governing body has been accused by the Sudanese of supporting rebel groups in Darfur. Chad claims heritage from what was once a paradise. Chad wants to mean, *Come all who are weary and drink.*

The Aging Rock Star

doesn't fit in anywhere. Even mowing the lawn he looks like a near-extinct animal—hairy, muscled forearms. Dyed-black hair hanging limp as brussel sprouts. Ordering a sandwich in the small-town deli, his bracelets clatter against each other, and his sandpaper face makes him look like maybe he was never loved enough. Cheering on his little girl from the soccer bleacher seats, fist pumping, he's like an Old Testament prophet, political activist, Ozzy Osbourne, Neil Young. No one knows what to say to him. He still seems to be dancing to the beats of his old drummer, even though his best days have sagged like an old roof, a sprung bed, middle-aged gut. Once upon a time he must've been someone to contend with, a figure rousing crowds to fury, then setting them free. He seems to be released from whatever propped him up those years of his youth. Wears black tee shirts of local bands even when he sometimes goes to church, clicking down the sidewalk in snakeskin boots, singing broken hosannas to himself, or anyone who'll listen.

Screenplay Plot for *A Walking Cliché Coins a Phrase*

He's like Everyman. So, he walks into a bar and says, "Howdy Blue Eyes," to the first woman he sees. She ignores him. The bartender asks, "What'll it be, Stranger?" "Anything on the rocks, shaken." That's for the comedy. The woman gets up and walks to a booth, lights up a slim cigarette. He struts to the retro jukebox, selects *Desperado*, *The Joker*, and last but not least, *Stairway to Heaven*. He sings along in wistful passion as the crescendo builds. Another man sits down next to the woman and they point and laugh at him. He slaps his money on the counter, chokes down his drink, and walks out without so much as *Goodbye*, just a fare-thee-well tip of the cap.

So this Cliché, let's call him _____, he wants to travel all over, start a band, cut a CD. He has an alacrity for blues riff, catchy lyrics, the pentatonic scale and three-chord pop songs sung with feeling and harmony. But his world falls apart when he breaks his leg and collarbone. Picture a skiing accident—almost fatal—and at first the leg won't heal. He takes to drinking and cracking fat jokes about his wife to her face. The break-up scene—his middle-age wife, a big brunette, fifth-grade teacher yells that he's "Lazy and good for nothing." He says, "I could care less." "Don't you mean you *'couldn't* care less'?" she screams. "If you cared, Bob, you'd at least learn to speak correctly." Leaves him. He throws a bottle of red wine and it explodes against the door a split second after she slams it. That's symbolic of him being like, "Good riddance!"

Then _____ tries to get smart and politically engaged. He flies to a Libertarian thinktank. This is the political intrigue. They preach private charity will shift the global structure. *Like they can conquer the Free World. A slice for everyone.* He thinks he gets it. But then in the climactic scene he interrupts the speaker, yells, "Get a piece of the pie!" The others turn to him. It gets quiet. He's planned to make this big speech but blanks out, and as he starts to faint, he points to the flip chart, says "The proof's in the pudding."

They drag him out. They think he's nuts. The speaker clears his throat.

Final scene: The cocktail conversation afterwards brims with fresh ideas, jokes, everyone saying something original or witty. He wakes up and limps outside for a walk feeling like the rebel outsider he fears he will always be. He watches the leaves falling from the Michigan trees in October. Slow piano melody. He starts to have this kind of epiphany. He carves his name among the graffiti initials and hearts and arrows. The wind knocks his GAP cap off and he chases it down a Hollywood Main Street. It blows onto a doorstep. He bends to pick it up, and a beautiful blonde opens the door. He thinks, *this was meant to be*, but decides to play it safe and pulls in the reins. She invites him in. After a meatloaf to die for, she says something cute like "Take me to the moon or lose me forever." He adds, "We'll wish on falling stars." She giggles. *Happily ever after*, he thinks, unbuckling his belt. Fade to a calendar blowing pages into the future, and them 30 years later, eating turkey with the family.

Day in the Life

Today I get up with you, watch you towel your hair, apply base, eyeliner, lipstick. Mostly I examine the birthmark on the left cheek just below the dimple. Your mark looks like an exotic country, Mongolia or Venezuela, with a couple of scattered islands. When you were a girl it was at the top of your thigh, but over the years it crested your flesh, made its way near the column of vertebrae. I love it because of its intimacy, because not everyone has a birthmark in the shape of Venezuela or Mongolia on her left cheek. I'm trying to think of what history I might know of those two countries, Simon Bolivar, *El Liberador* of Venezuela, the conquering Khan dynasty, nomadic hordes of Mongolia, decimating European armies back in the 14th century. There is the history the world knows and the one forever hidden from view.

Notes from Jesus

I tell Jesus something is worrying me and troubling my mind. Jesus says the bleeding from my wrists is natural to one with faith like mine. Jesus says to consider the lilies of the field. Jesus says it's His will being done. Jesus tells me not to be afraid. "Love your neighbor" He says, and I do. Sometimes I love my neighbor by bringing brownies. Sometimes I wave. Jesus says "It's the little things that count." I tell Jesus I agree. Jesus says "I am the Way the Truth the Light." Jesus tells me I have the Way the Truth the Light and that no one comes to the Father except through what I know because I know that He's my deep down feeling and that's the Way the Truth the Light. Jesus highlights the most edifying verses. Jesus says He's blessed our nation. Jesus says we'd better give unto Caesar what's his. I tell Jesus the power bill is too high and it's hard to give and still buy reasonable gifts for the family but Jesus is so patient with me. He shakes his head with those big blue eyes and calls me Child because we're all children in Jesus' eyes. He says "For I alone know the plans I have for you, plans to make you prosper and not to suffer." Jesus says the suffering of other nations is because of their lack of moral vision is because they don't have the Way the Truth the Light. Jesus says he's come not to bring peace but a sword. Jesus says the poor we'll always have. Jesus says we see through a glass darkly. Jesus says we'll know more after the Tribulation and the suffering of other nations will only have just begun. Jesus says those chain letters are usually false prophets. It says "Something is troubling me and worrying my mind." Jesus says I might have a good word for this person because something has been troubling me and worrying my mind. Jesus says I wouldn't want to brake the chain.

Seven Lightning Strikes

Strike #1

No one to see how his eyes had been on the waving pine boughs as the ump raised his hands and the players hustled in. No one to him just a few beats behind, as he crossed the infield just past second base. No one to see his every hair stand on end. A flash as quick as an eyeblink, thunder booming in the chest. No light shown in his eyes. Only his boots blown halfway to first as if he'd leapt ahead of himself.

Strike #2

He doesn't tell anyone his heart flutters, his ears ring. The strike means he was born to preach. People flock to him. The Itinerant Miracle. Witness the Man Who Lived Thru Lightning. Lazarus in the Flesh. He's baptizing a young believer in the river outside Palm Beach. "Luck," he bellows to the multitudes, "is just another word for fate." *Amen.* "We all have mountains to climb." *Preach on.* "I baptize you in the name—" A dazzle of light. The girl shudders in his arms, passes on to the Second Birth. He can't feel his body as he carries the girl's to shore.

Strike #3

Hammering, this time, out of the open blue. Right in the middle of the duck boat like a bolt from Zeus. When he wakes he feels his hairless arms, smooth brow—the knot of burned flesh on his scapula. He remembers it like a dream. Fish swimming just beneath the surface, the water lucid. He closes his eyes and sees the stripes on the bass, can almost count the spots on the freckled bream. In the mirror, he sees the eyelashes are gone too. *How like the hairless creatures of creation we are,* he thinks.

Strike #4

How much more miraculous is he now? A man struck down by 300 kilovolts three times, a man still on the right path? This time during the Invitation at a revival in downtown Minneapolis. No rain. Just people waving their hands, some swooning, some speaking in tongues. Only wind gusting off the river and across Memorial Hill. No thunder warning. Quick, sudden, like death to Ananias. Blasts him backwards out of his Samsonite metal folding chair, right out of his toenails. When he rises again from the hospital table after minor surgery, the dumbstruck town rejoices.

Strike #5
Hell's Canyon, Idaho. Through his pick-up's window—a direct blow to the temple, his hair blazes hot and fast like dry pine. He says, *I saw the beast who comes from the Euphrates and the many heads of the European Union and strange flowers blooming on Megidda. An angel struck me with his rod. With each blow he yelled out a name, each one standing for the twelve tribes of Israel. The angel said it stands for all who cannot contain the words of terror which reign in the hearts and minds of men. He said if the rulers of this age understood God's wisdom they would not crucify the Lord of Glory again.*

Strike #6
Golfing on July 4th at 4:00 in the afternoon in Panama, Florida. The most likely time and place to be struck on the planet. He has nothing to lose. No one can believe how he goes on living. His fiancé fans herself in the golf cart. The nine iron flies from his white glove which flies from his outstretched hands which flies from his thumbnails. His fiancé leaves him, says she needs space. "Thank you," he says to the nurse, coming in with food from the hospital cafeteria. "You're a lucky man," she says.

Strike #7
"Not all who wander are lost," he says. He drops a clay pot on the stage. It shatters to smithereens. Lightning blows through the stained-glass window. His body seizes. His white robes flutter. Someone says, "O my God." Someone says to call 911. His robe is singed black. They're carrying him away on a stretcher when he opens his eyes and says, "Who will pick up the vessel's pieces?" I re-dedicate my life on the spot. He shoots himself in the heart the next day. Three lead fingers from a .22. They say from losing in love. They say a lot of funny things.

2   The End of the World

The End of the World

He'd been to the End of the World and it *wasn't all that*. He wanted something more than a couple of placid sheep, a small valley, a few shops selling pocketknives and cheese. It's not that he really thought he'd find anything *Apocalyptic*. It's just that he wants wonders—trees growing through rocks, a valley of bones, a lake of fire, shepherds hunkered down looking for the North Star's guiding light. He'd listened to false prophets before but had managed to keep working like a True Disciple, predicted the Day of the Lord, called it divine and flew to the compound. He saw lilies blooming in the desert, fires carving through the northwest. But the government refused to recognize the Savior, bore down on the followers with tanks and M-16s. He had to peer through binoculars, snap a whip at the tee shirt stand to cleanse the area for a New Temple. God shined a great white eye, and the Savior went up in a host of flames. Now he alone is left.

Three Rose Tattoo

Even permanent ink stretches and fades, gains and loses meanings like the red that drains from three roses on his deltoid as he labors in the heat painting houses without a shirt the summer he turns nineteen—the green leaves of the roses, highlighted with yellow, now dun. The band was set on making a bond though they'd never played beyond a garage. Just sixteen, beads of sweat form on his brow and lips as the buzzing instrument weaves repeatedly the first small petal, and soon he numbs, stares glassy-eyed at their swaggering lead singer, Frank, fresh from the black leather seat, a babe in high-heel boots taking up half his left arm. The drunk artist, Lizard, with a Byzantine Jesus taking up half his back, promises discounts for women to draw on. The bruised sun mixes in the clouds and sets behind the Exxon sign before the drummer and guitarist get their turn. They seem relieved, but say they'll get their tatts next week. The band drives home with the top down on Frank's '57 Chevy. They break up a few days later, disagreeing over the set list of Metal tunes they'll play at Battle of the Bands. So now he makes up stories about his roses. To his frat friends, a jailhouse tatt and he was paroled before they drew in guns. To his teachers, a metaphor for loss. To girls, he might've said they were a sign for their lifelong love. To his son, a birthmark that never faded.

Rehearsing

It's dark down the highway even with the brights on. In the rain the streetlights aren't much help either. A million drops splashing on the road and windshield. The future rock star and Destiny pull over every few hours to pour water down the radiator before they're blinded by the steam, overheating, like their love, and on the brink of collapse, taking unscheduled pit stops. What keeps them driving is the Seattle Sound, the hard licks of unclean acid, hallucinations of fame and fortune thrumming like electric currents in their tired brains. They make it just in time for the headliners. Before they know it, Cobain jumps into the pit. They carry him on their shoulders, touch the hem of his sweaty shirt. Afterwards they get married. But everything since then, the rest of their lives, seems like the doldrums of the humming highway—the distance between Pocatello and Portland. He keeps rehearsing for another stolen moment. He'll know it when it hits. He'll grab on to that rising wheel of glory just like before—a someone—dancing, smashed, careening, amplified.

Muted Blues Bird

Tomorrow, he's back on the road, so tonight, he begins her with a simple 1-4-5. She's his cherry-top *Takemine*, his *baby*, curvy, broken-in, his ax to grind, his instrument to improvise on—reproducing only the best songs from her belly. Plugged in, amplified, she feels lit, electric, like music kicking up in her bones and through her body's hollow, and then she's no longer gazing up at the ceiling mirror, but down upon the two of them, and hears, faint, from the other room, the muted bird chirping inside the chimney where it's made the mistake of making a nest. The poor bird's root note sounds like a 7th, a question, suggestion of restlessness, of having arrived at the end of a long flight, only to find the song coming out wasn't right, wasn't the way she thought the song would sound like coming out.

Letter to Plant from Easter Island

Dear Robert,

Once upon a time this island was the End of the World, and right now, as a man claiming lineage to its ancient people preaches about misunderstood Polynesian belief, I'm reminded of a photo I'd stare at for hours in my youth of you peering over Phoenix in 1971, arms spread wide on your third American tour, only 22—a year before my birth. You yelled, "I'm a golden god!" Now that I'm excoriating the dream of my past, I'm coming to terms with my old gods. I still go back and turn up the volume, and imagine a glory of golden locks blossoming like a wild garden from my head, bracelets rattling, and a kind of wailing rising from the depths of my divided soul. If only I could topple the totems of my dreams like the monolithic Moai of Easter Island, and let the lineage of truth's traceable ancestor erase the past's lava rock. I don't have anything against you, Robert. I really only know you by your warbling. You're like Zeus—not a god but a story—who looked down on a brave world, lightning bolt in hand, and had nowhere to go but down. We want to believe our gods will fail so we can prove they aren't any more joyful than we are. My version of the White Lady is that she's preposterous, posthumous love; love that leaves a bruise in the shape of a rose; love like a distorted amp revving through the suburbs of my past.

Letter to (Un)Resurrected Messiah

Why won't you answer? Call me recalcitrant, but I'm beginning to have doubts that literal miracles, like you floating free from the compound's fire, really happen. Quarantine my hard heart, but all I want is to touch you, hear back. Is it too much to ask for a drink together? Fill me up with love like that. *Invade me. Come inside. Ravish. Have your own way.* How about a vision? Package it with a migraine if you like and some mysterious lesson on suffering. Speak prophetic in my inner ear. I tell you what, unless I hear otherwise, I'm going back to the Davidian compound to find the lost tablets. I'll take an old DC-10 and breathe some life into it. I'll fly it into Tajikistan—they'll take it as a sign, a luminary explosion in the heart of the terrorist's training camps. They'll worship from my black hole. Wild poppies will bloom as a symbol for orgiastic glee. They'll find my letters in the blackbox recorder. They'll found the New True Religion, or whatever you call them to. Through me others can change the world, one ignorant infidel after another. The whole earth can start over, a whole linked chain of the right DNA, towering to the satellites of Heaven. Please write back, I'm a mustard seed for your love.

Where Prevost was Conceived

Chad Prevost was born in Marin General Hospital in Fairfax, California which was the same hospital that Robin Williams was born in. It's quite possible that other famous and funny people were born in Marin General Hospital. In fact, the chances are quite good. Prevost only knows about Robin Williams though. Prevost learned about this innocent little fact at a relatively early age and it seems to have had a strange impact on him. It may have been due to the fact that Prevost's father mentioned this fact to him on a long drive back from his grandfather's lake house, and took the long drive to discuss masturbation and the ways men and women have intercourse. This was the language his father used, presumably because it is biblical. Prevost was eight. For a long time Prevost thought Robin Williams, playing the character Mork in *Mork and Mindy*, was really an alien from another planet who was quite kind to others if a little awkward and had a funny handshake Prevost would try to emulate on others throughout his adolescence even long after *Mork and Mindy* had gone off the air. The image of birth was only reinforced when Prevost bought a pack of trading card stickers at Paradise Pharmacy of various celebrities of one kind or another which contained a sticker-card with the image of Mork emerging in a space suit from a giant egg. Prevost liked to keep the sticker-cards more as cards and not as stickers, but even at an early age Prevost was prone to impulsive decisions and during this time Prevost chose to stick all his stickers wherever he could. He stuck the image of Mork emerging from a giant egg on the front cover of his fourth grade, three-ring binder where he stared at it for long hours. When Prevost was 15, having long since moved off to the East Coast due to his father's receiving a call from God, Prevost's father took Prevost back across the country to his native soil for reasons Prevost no longer recalls. Prevost's father drove Prevost straight from the airport to the Golden Gate Theological Seminary, pulled into a narrow parking space and pointed at a narrow end-unit off Strawberry Landing, Apartment 1B. Prevost's father lead Prevost in. "You were conceived in this room. Right here, in this very bed." The room was pallid gray, filtered light blinked through the blinds. A flood of guilt and embarrassment swept over Prevost as he envisioned the way this intimacy had taken shape. Prevost felt strangely honored that he'd be shown where he was conceived, but at the same time as if this was perhaps too personal a detail to have revealed—at least from one's own father. Prevost's first thought was the baby Jesus, but Prevost felt much less special than Jesus who at least had been born in a manger with donkeys and goats and wise men bearing gifts. Prevost was conceived in a unit. A headache began to set in like a dull throb, and Prevost had an image of the narrator in the "Tell-Tale Heart." He peered in at the stripped, queen-sized mattress, wide window with blinds turned down but the sun beaming through and casting sharp horizontal lines running across the room. Dust floated like paramecium in the thick air. "Right here?" Prevost asked. Prevost's father stood over him, proudly, as if the significance of this moment Prevost would surely comprehend. "Right here." Then, Prevost began to feel something birthing inside him, a new understanding, shuddering, cracking, splitting open. Prevost wasn't exactly sure what he was seeing in his mind's eye, whether it was Prevost's own self, or God's Son, or perhaps even Robin Williams; all he could make out was a small, dark head crowning through a giant egg in the strangely shadowed room.

Poem Escaping through Holes in the Ozone

This cloudy poem achieves new heights in self-reference even its author has no idea where it's floating off to while already in the thin air above the ungrounded context of millions of poems this one has the audacity to float above the hot air balloons with its personified ears popping and not even its speaker has anything more than a dim recollection of the jet graveyard the poem in question now refers to having witnessed while lost looking for the tunnels of the eviscerated Branch Davidian Compound where the officials would never have permitted it to reach a reader in the real world except for a satellite having photographed the treatment of this odd poem's orbiting in the past so unaware of the futility of its very existence it would be off the record without a trace and whatever it might have said about matter and meaning or to how the holes got so big as to let it slide through in the first place could've been denied and labeled as irrelevant other than being grounded in a fleeting moment at the relative beginning of a whole millennia's worth of second chances as unguided as ever as powerless to stop trying to keep from floating

3 The Book of Masters

Dear Order and Meaning,

I've lined up the dominoes of consent upon your doorstep. I've mowed the lawn and trimmed the rose of Sharon. I'm singing on the shores of your carbon-dated desert that once was a sea. The genius in this is that it already was an ocean bottom. Already I can breathe here under the tutelage of its white sands, the sun beaming down like an icon of mystery, and me, on an ordinary Sunday like this, can sip at the mirage of my Cocteau supreme fiction. Quit your peacock preening—nothing is so exacting as your illusions. Even the sea knew when to stop its ceasless chatter.

Dear Narrowing Gyre,

How tight do events need to wheel back upon themselves before anyone learns? How many falconers? How many thorns their roses? How many broken towers, raped Ledas? Your sand's dance is no longer anything but a wild whirling that no one can understand. How many nooses? How many tongues? How many ears? I'm a megalopolis for your future. I'm a minivan for your good suburb people. I need a new symbol system. Let's make what stands hold its step, move in rhythm, bleed among the lapis lazuli and schoolchildren's aging hearts.

Letter to Zarathustra from Hypochondriac

Dear Zarathustra in Love,
My alter ego is full of himself. He too has peered into the pistol's black hole, the Grand Canyon's Eastern Rim at night till he almost fell into himself. Then he got himself together, shaved, took a shower, took rejection as a gift. For he so loved the world he littered the world with solicitations enough to rent his paper heart. He found himself with a flair for the dramatic, painting Adara's name in glowing neon across his chest, wading waist deep in the Ohio, noodling for catfish with his bare hands, and singing when he found a mouth that bit him. *My heart bleeds for you Penelope* draped across the toll bridge, painted with ink from the Mississippi and blood drawn straight from his left side. I wish I could stop him but he's in love with everything Greek, ancient and otherwise. He studied Burton's *Anatomy of Melancholy*, empathized with the man's great personal pain that drove him to write by a flickering candlelight about hypochondriacs and the pathology of certain death. *Hypo* meaning "the body." *Chondria* meaning "of the ribs." Zarathustra, is it true? Nothing really matters so we might as well fall in love? Is it true what a broken heart can do: cleanse despair's black bile of a world swirling up the tubes? If we all get painted over then paint the town black? If so, he's on board and he's taking me with him: jumping ship, drowning with you and all the world's super-egos, laughing at the sorrow that breaks our hearts.

Letter to Jordan from an Economy-Sized Best Western

Dear Mike,
Once, I put my hand in your hand's imprint at a Foot Locker in Chicago. No wonder your hand spans the ball's circumference! Mike, you've become so big you might as well be slamming us home through Time's net. That's my slant anyway. I know another side of the truth might prove you're just another aging athlete passing a little ungracefully into the oblivion of gravity's constant tug. I don't see it that way any more than I see greatness as being anything but un-rebounded from the jump shot of our lives. Just take those hooped earrings dangling from your symmetrical lobes, or that Nike icon—a silhouette of you, legs spread, arm cocked like a trigger about to unload on an innocent basket all the fury against being merely good enough. And that tongue you never bite though it curls outside your mouth in the melee against hapless opponents who only push you higher as they flail against your highness! The glory of you is that you'll always be present tense, leaping toward a goal above the rest of our average heads, the ball palmed in a single hand. Mike, no one wants to be average, but how many of us have any idea what it would be like to be so far above the rim of ordinary mortals as to cast a shadow too long to see the end of? I have some footage of you somewhere, smiling your youthful smile in a light blue Tar Heel uniform. You're spinning the ball on a single finger so fast it starts to have that look of spinning backwards—Mike, the globe pivots on your fingertip.

Letter to Bonds from Savings and Loan

Dear Barry,

Please excuse the informal nature of this note, I just want you to know I'm a fan and there are at least some of us who have your best interests at heart. We appreciate your using us as a repository of financial savings for safety deposit relics like the jersey you wore when you clobbered #715 over the wall. As you no doubt know, our bank originated here in the epicenter of this city's district: survived the quake of 1906. You don't remember it I know, but back when you weren't even in the 500 club you signed my son's ball. In my book you're the King—forgiving them who do not understand. I get it: I wouldn't want to please the media hounds either. You don't smile at them the right way and they cast you as some kind of villain. They twist and dig into your words. Whatever they say, what happens on that field is real. You're living every man's fantasy. They can't accept the fact that some of us were born to break new ground. Please take this letter as an off-the-record note just between your broker and you. My covenant with you is my word: you keep hitting them out and I'll keep buying in.

Letter to a Suicide Letter

Jeremy,
You bolted from treatment at Memorial and picked up where you'd left off—on the road with anyone following the Dead, *looking for a miracle*. An expert hitcher for a guy who once owned a Volvo. Your letter is one long string of names and ours are on it. Are they goodbyes or a list of everyone who failed you? Your last New Year night you asked, "Don't you think it's strange that Morrison, Hendrix, Bonham and Joplin all OD-ed, were our age, and had 'J' in their first name?" Did we answer without thinking? "It immortalized them," my brother said. Summer nights you'd take us downtown, avoiding interstates, under the bridge on Krog with its lamp-lit graffiti moons and lips, through alleys we've yet to find again, acquainting us with Atlanta: the underground scene, neon palaces, hammered girls. Next spring you'd fallen apart—quit your job, went missing with two rich dudes from Japan, enough coke to last a lifetime, touring the country in their Mercedes following rave scenes and jam bands. Then they find you in the basement hanging from a pipe? My brother had a star by his name—John*. Where do I send this letter, Jeremy? The songs go on every day, dude, every day. Sometimes we take a joy ride, crank your music, and squeal donuts in the parking lots where we all slugged beers and peeled away, the burning rubber hot in our noses. Jeremy, you loser. Those who love you, love you regardless.

Break-Up Letter under the Influence

Dear Jack n' Coke,
We can call it a white lie if you want, but sometimes you make me feel like you're thinking about moving in. That scares me. I mean, you do get me feeling *so good*; you make me want to love my neighbor. Just lately, you've had me believing in the love and loyalty of my friends. Sometimes I do need that. You bring a need to make the world more relaxed, to talk of things I'd have no energy for otherwise. If only the world's leaders had more like you, they might let a few more sanctions slide. It's true, even as I break up with you I'm telling you you're capable of anything—changing world policy even. Jack, I must admit, I swim in your fibs. My gills fan you in and out. It's the coming back up that never works out. You love me then you leave me. Now, don't go getting soft and sappy. By now I know you're just the whiskey talking. There's no use being friends—but while you're here—you want one last parting squeeze?

Dear I Am Already a Mountain Range,

Even the horses pull in opposite directions beneath you, dismembering the tectonic plates you believe have nothing to do with you. How much pressure can a single range take before its rivers slice open its soft belly? Might as well say I'm already squeezing the water out of this sand. Might as well chalk it up to a weather pattern circling around your peak's thin air: too much rain and cold, not enough tender hooks, lovebird songs. Look, even mountains go bald, all those hardwood cherries blighting like a receding tree line across your stony forehead.

Dear Light Those at Work See,

You are the ever-changing color of yellow to red to green and back again. You cut yourself through my office's single-window blind. Your florescence provides the effervescent parade of shapes on my retinal screen. There you are again, glowing through the opaque windows in the men's restroom. You are my tie glowing at my throat in a half-windsor knot.

Letter from Branch Manager of Terminal Accounts, Division 3

Dear customer 3535 4120 4642 8850:
Our records indicate you have paid off your balance and would like to terminate this credit line. Please find your confirmation number enclosed. I'd like to remind you of the advantages of carrying our card as protection against all manner of catastrophe. Each dollar you spend with your card, for instance, goes to fight the war of your choice: terror, hunger, cancer, to name a few. Our records indicate you've had some close calls: the time your parachute failed to open. I can just imagine the cord stringing behind you like a dead jellyfish. Our records don't indicate how you survived, only hospital records reporting a broken femur of soldier 88932150, Honorably Discharged some 23 days later. Our records do indicate a series of one-bedroom flats up and down the Eastern seaboard. Your account has had a pattern of accumulating vast sums only to disappear. I'm only Branch Manager of Terminal Accounts, Division 3, but your account would seem to have a kind of tidal flow, floods and droughts, that sort of thing, which—I'm just noting facts—is sometimes indicative of gambling. Perhaps you're one who likes the odds against him? I'd like to think of this credit line as a defense against incurring more trouble. Off the record, the House always wins. Please accept our Fire Protection Policy and Life Insurance coverage for such an enduring customer. Did you know the turnover rate for a job like mine is among the highest bracket? 62% don't last two years. 54% have heart attacks within five. We have a 27% higher suicide rate than dentists and 41% higher than poets, according to the U.S. Bureau of Statistics. Once I cast my fate to the wind and played Russian Roulette but that was before my new life: a reliable wife and two girls off to college. I've lived a paint-by-the-numbers life I guess someone like you might say, but who would've kept track of you? Thank you again for following through with your financial obligations. I suppose life itself is a trail of trial and error. That's why we have parachutes like credit to keep you from breaking should you find yourself falling. Please do consider yourself fortunate, as I do, having tracked you all these years.

4 What Volcanologists Know

Notes Toward What Volcanologists Know

Be wary of the thing you love. Tread lightly, with the deference of one approaching a god. Your god may only seem asleep. A volcanologist knows the difference between pyroclastic flows and caldera collapses, has danced on Hawaiian Islands, magma seeping into the blue. A volcanologist knows terrains that do not seem like the earth at all, knows the way steam rises from pumice, enveloping in dark grooves like the human heart. She's not afraid, she just knows things can spew at any given moment. A volcanologist knows 120 Celsius is the temperature at which hair singes, even from 15 miles away over 900-foot ridges. She feels she's been spared because she's lived to see Mount Saint Helens by falling into a root ball, trees collapsing like toothpicks above her. She has risked a look through the cracks after long silence, to see the sky clear and ash begin to fall. A volcanologist knows the earth will change, but she can't get everything out of her mind—like how heat mummifies a body from an eruption 15 miles away, the muscle cooking, and the way afterwards while she waited for help, it looked like water was splitting from rocks of the exploding mountain. Volcanologists have no fantastical visions—they see what they see. They'll compare a volcano to a launching NASA rocket, artillery, a steam locomotive, or will describe how one can taste sulfur dioxide at a certain temperature. They'll say, "exceptionally loud," "inaudible shocks," "temporary deafness," "ash and pumice particles falling through the forest," "intellectual tools to interpret," "the present is key to the past." A volcanologist knows what it means to risk everything for a single fact, measures her chances, like the graduation of heat beneath her toes, with seismographs and the odds that one burst will follow previous patterns.

On the Identity Formation of Prevost

Chad Prevost was born a second time at Tiburon Baptist Church, overlooking Angel Island. By the time he was 16 his parents called him a searching Christian. In Sunday School Prevost learned Brianna's truth of Chakras and the body's layered pleasure points. Brianna said, "We have one soul. For some it takes thousands of lives to get it right." Prevost was enchanted. He followed her, noticed the way she wobbled on her heels. Brianna's alcoholic grandfather wasn't home when, second date, she opened the door dressed in black lingerie. She called him her white prince, lead him to the claw-foot tub lit up with so many candles Prevost found himself feeling a sense of the sacred, like he should be kneeling in prayer instead of kneeling eye-level with her belly. All summer she had Prevost fumbling over his power chords, seeking divine guidance. She steered with her thighs the wheel of his white Vega, rolling jays of exotic weed from dealers she never let Prevost meet. The hiss-and-pop audio of Widespread Panic bootlegs reeled into Prevost's dreams. Prevost meditated with her daily, a crystal poised between his eyes—experiencing past versions of his soul's habitation. He found himself peering through the eyes of John, baptizing Sweet Jesus Himself, God's voice thundering overhead, a dove cooing in an olive tree. Once he thought about nothing for so long he actually lifted off the ground. Mostly, though, Prevost just found himself hungering for Brianna's transfigured body. Her nails raking across his back, the two of them screaming and sweating like gods creating a world. Prevost's mother asked him where the stray red marks across his back had come from when he momentarily lapsed and took off his shirt to mow the lawn. "Ah, sticks or something," was the best Prevost could come up with. His mother nodded and looked away and walked back inside. Brianna left Prevost to go on a dig outside the Petrified Forest with a divorced Archaeology professor who once called her brilliant. Prevost dreamed them groaning among the ruins of some nomadic Apache tribe littered with brittle bone and broken arrowheads dating back to the otherwise neglected past. Brianna wrote to Prevost years later, asking him to join her at a nudist colony where they ran in circles on public land, holding hands, chanting to the river, asking to be taken back in. Prevost was intrigued but by this time had re-dedicated his life and was currently serving as a part-time janitor at Columbus Avenue Baptist Church while studying Hebrew and attending his seminary classes regularly.

Bowing Not Knowing to What

At the fundraiser for the youth mission trip we bowed to pray by the softball field, tipped our caps, listened to the wind and the crickets, played graceless ball for six innings and a scoreboard full of runs and errors. By the Brazos River we bowed for Rebel, who, on Thanksgiving Day weighted himself down and plunged below Suspension Bridge. In the mission house on an anonymous avenue that spilled congregants down a root-split sidewalk, we bowed for jobs, for the Holy Ghost to heal Fernando who slipped on a mop and broke his back. Mostly I'd just stay in, study and stare out the window, sometimes all night, waiting for a sign or for the blond across the street to rip open her blinds, strip, cover herself with milk and honey.

A Walking Cliché Tries Not to Peek at the Cleavage of His Foreign-Exchange Student Who Says Her Grandmother Was a Persian Princess

Her body is a temple where men come to bow and he can see her saying to the boyfriend she's just made love to, whose hands have touched every sacred place, "All good things come to an end" like the drama-queen she is, fulfilling the script of wistful romance, "but the memories we'll always have." How many times was he that boy when a fling ended with those very words whispered through the last gasp of a late telephone call or sitting for the last time on the edge of her damp bed? It's a cross-cultural lesson—when faced with the half-hidden fruit outside the garden where one was once prone to wander, the road splits without warning—avert the eyes, think of St. John of the Cross becoming ego-less as a landscape of windswept dust, or bury oneself in sweetness like a bee making Heaven in a fallen pear?

For now he wanders the valley of the library like a lost Hebrew, breathing old apples as the sun goes down, a cleaved ego, peering up into the cloudy light at the mystic peaks. He thinks of a line from Chekhov he read years ago. "If you fear loneliness, then marriage is not for you," and a strange despair comes over him like a wool-hair habit, and he feels again how imperfect this condition will always be. He dreams of shapes—slant of a shoulder meeting the delicate neckline, arc of a waist meeting hip, curve of a lip taking back its shape after a hard kiss. He finds himself sprinting to any dark space where he can give birth to the impenitent multitudes chanting within, praying for release, as he invites and shuts out the choirs singing of the majesty of silence, the dethronement of flesh.

Dear Life-size Muse,

For the record, I shrunk you down to the size you looked from my back window and took you with me everywhere only because I couldn't have you in the way that I believed would be—most satisfactory. For instance, the small circle of my guitar behind the strings, which I now realize might have looked like prison bars from inside. But how the walls of that guitar vibrated with you inside! And I know I could've been gentler when I shook you out like a fumbled pick but you have to admit how much fun we both had when I hung you from my rear-view mirror. With my crystal swinging light on my Vega's interior vinyl, I could look at you when the highway was free and open and REM jammed from the speakers. Do you still love REM? It was like you were dancing on a disco ball with the Rocky Mountains as your stage drop. I know it got hot in the car, but that's why I kept you in the top drawer of my desk where you clung to that red Crayola. Remember? Remember the moon? Remember how it looked through our empty pilsners from the Brazos River? Remember the Brazos and mooning the moon through our pilsners turned upside down? My friends thought they were losing me. What was I going off alone for all the time? Just a few weeks earlier we'd slug Pabst Blue Ribbon in front of the tube, play video games or watch *Killing Zoe*. Roger convinced the intellectually inferior Andrew that you and I were getting too close. They were the ones who spread the rumors. They knew you as the girl who lived behind me, whom I'd watch from my back window when she sunbathed in her yellow bikini. Before I knew it you'd grown life-sized and stood on my front porch, hands on your hips, looking flushed and beautiful as ever. But was it really necessary to bring along that meathead who grabbed me by the collar when I smiled and beat me like I'd never been beaten before? Look, I apologize for the miscommunication. Can we have the old times back, singing at the moon, racing reckless down the highway full of the closest thing to beer this county has to offer? Can I shrink you down again? So long as we never touch, will you always be my muse?

Chad Prevost Chases Chad Prevost to Make Sure the Future Comes True

Chad Prevost hails from Richmond, Virginia where he attended public schools in Henrico County's West End. Chad barely graduated from Mills E. Godwin High, and everyone who knew anything about Chad projected him as not particularly likely to succeed. Chad journeyed far and wide before returning nearly a decade later to attend his high school reunion. Chad ended up skipping the reunion because Chad heard his old Chevy wheezing down those West End suburban streets the very same day. Chad turned in to the apartment complex of his first mistaken love, the one who'd engraved his tattoo—three roses—on her Zippo. Chad sidled in through the sliding glass door and stood at the top of the stairs. If Chad had not seen Chad leaning against her blank white wall, black pillows propped behind him, Chad would probably not have believed it himself. Chad watched Chad set back the needle, listen to "Stairway to Heaven," and fiddle with his hair. "Don't scratch the vinyl," she yelled from the bathroom. "I won't live to see my fifteenth birthday," Chad said. "What baby?" she yelled over the hairdryer. "I said I'm going to die on a Thursday." The Chad watching Chad realized how similar this prediction sounded to one made by the famous Peruvian poet, Cesar Vallejo, but Chad also knew Chad had no knowledge of Vallejo. She came back in the room, tying back her hair. Chad had forgotten how young she was, and to have already lost a father and brother. No wonder she said simply, "Let's go have a smoke." Chad followed them out the door, and through thick traffic all the way downtown. Chad watched Chad kick at a loose rock and say, "It'll be a Thursday because Fridays Dad goes out of town. He needs to be in town." Chad followed at a reasonable distance as long as Chad could, past the Stonewall Jackson memorial, across Broad Street, toward the outskirts of Richmond. Chad and his girlfriend walked without any apparent direction, arm in arm. Then Chad turned around and saw Chad watching himself. Chad grabbed his girlfriend by the arm, hooking a sharp turn around the Booth Refrigeration and Supply warehouse, where Chad probably still punched in as a picker and had lunches at Picadilly with Wolf. Chad pursued, wanting to tell Chad things about a future he didn't believe in. "You'll study Theology," Chad yelled. "You'll fall in love with poetry and many women. Your rock star illusions will never come true but you'll have children and they will ground you." Chad had no way of knowing whether they heard him. A few minutes later Chad reported hearing sirens wailing down Shepard Street. Chad followed the sirens, and couldn't believe his good fortune. There was Chad dashing down steps into the basement of an old factory. Chad ran to catch up, bursting into a dark room. Chad was just in time to glimpse Chad's black Chuck Taylors at the top of a wobbly staircase. Chad pursued, stumbling. Chad could hear himself running up and up, flight after flight until Chad came to an enormous room of rotting cloth and old Singers, a room filled with light from all the tall and broken windows. "You'll have to believe there's more," Chad yelled. Then Chad heard the groan and squeal of the fire escape. Chad ran to a window in time to see Chad abandoning Chad's self, letting go some twenty feet off the ground, hitting the uneven sidewalk with a slap, running for his life, toward a future no one would ever predict.

The Dead Among Us

Every night you can hear them hammering on the door, drunk, waiting to be let in, forgiven for past sins, tripping a light or shuddering in the wind. You can hear them singing together, arm in arm. Sometimes you can even look out your window and see them kick at cans or toe the sand from a swing that never swings, just sways. Sometimes you can hear them letting their guns blaze, taking cover behind magnolias and Cadillacs. The dead aren't holding anything back. They are living out their lives. We hear them but think, *thunder, lightning, wind in the pines, a car backfiring.* Better to roll over in your warm bed, ignore the moonlight peering through the shades.

Baptism by Fire

What I remember is my father asking to be forgiven for sacrificing so much family time teaching the sinners what they needed saving from. I remember him pounding the pulpit preaching, jaws clenched, brow lifted, stabbing at the air.

I remember Adam and I were killing a Saturday on the marsh banks at low tide, witnessing what the high tide kept hidden—bed frames, beer bottles, coffee cans, shoes stuck in sludge. We hauled a tire up to the small shore, fed an oily rag inside its center. I'd stolen matchbooks from my mother's collection. I lit the rag. Flames leapt like an animal desperate to escape, the head-high wheat by the banks the fuel for its departure. For a moment I stopped pedaling away, and turned to the wind-fed blaze. I'd never seen anything so beautiful and ravenous, eating every hidden thing—rattlesnakes, raccoons, gophers, grackles scattering like thrown pepper. The fire licked at my heels by the highway curb. It was as if I were eye-to-eye with a vision from hell, sirens wailing, heat rising above homes.

What I remember is, still out of breath, lying to the Fire Chief who'd followed us. I blamed it on Adam. My mother discovered the truth. She found missing matchbooks and I confessed first to her, then my father, then the police who showed me snapshots of burned kids. My father dealt seven licks, forbid me to return to the marsh, or to leave home for what seemed at the time as a kind of eternity. Released a few weeks later, I rode to the marsh—black, vast, scarred, there was nothing left.

What I remember is holding my breath, bubbles rising, a glass-fronted tank of greenish water. The good news is I walked up the baptistery steps, a dead rose pinned to my sopping robe that clung to my small body. I was born again. How many times have I been forgiven since I was seven? How many times reborn, returning to that tank, burning, out of breath, burning?

5 Insomniac

Where the Light is Still Good

You have learned to step inside yourself, lay across empty spaces spreading like a blank canvas imprinted by what it touches, and going back, days or years later, changing the details, thinning them into tapestries of water colored worlds; dense purple-shadowed mountains, blue alcoves with broken windmills spinning one way then another along thunderous roads without guardrails where lightning splits like a wishbone. The sky empties itself of water as if saying that all things sad are what you have to live on, the make-up of your body, and two-thirds of the earth's surface. Here, where two moons rise together and rip apart over the curved mountain which looks like a woman lying on her back, you huddle in silence because for now all that needs saying has been said. Here, where the light is still good enough to see your shape, in this field of grass and stippled dirt, crooked joshua trees and cedar dotting the surface. You float like the scent of eucalyptus to the sky, leaving your body behind, dreaming things you mostly forget, the wings inside yourself extending.

What is Today?

Out the window exhaust spills to the sky, plumes of cars spinning their wheels. Yesterday was not so different. Tomorrow I'll write my name across the Marlboro billboard in flaming calligraphy. People will look up and follow the smoke. They'll see my name in flame against a razor blue sky. No sooner will it turn to ash than I'll cast myself from the highway's bridge into the Chickamauga Dam. I'll be waterskiing away by the time the Coast Guard arrives. They'll call me the Alleged Eco-Terrorist, accuse me of reading *Adbusters*. Amber alerts will pitch my license plate across the interstate as the man who kidnapped himself. I'll taxi all the way to Trump's Manhattan Tower. Maybe I won't have to hold a gun to Trump's head to persuade him to fly me to Rhode Island. O the view is fantastic today atop the country's cultural Mecca. We have to use the high beams to see through the smog which confuses the pigeons who don't know whether it's day or night. They careen between the blades. The engine sputters. We crash in a wheat field somewhere in what must be rural New Jersey: swampland but I can hear the wave of mass transit. Fighter jets blaze overhead. By the time they trace the smoke, I'm hitching a ride with Shareefa. She sports a Taco Bell uniform. "You don't know who I am?" I ask. "I don't watch much TV," she says. "Take me to the border," I say. "Ha ha," she says. I tell her I'm serious. Today's her lucky day. We're wheeling into the arms of love, into tomorrow's fantasy of how it all used to be. We stop in Cleveland for a shake, rob a liquor store in Kansas City. We steal the show in Branson, Missouri, where, magically, she gets herself spliced in two. Even as they cast my name in red letters on the Bijou Theater placard, I complete my disappearing act: grow a moustache, apply self-tanning lotion, volunteer to help build the wall from Baja to El Paso. I change my name to Homero, work with other Illegals building the wall from Mexico. But before I know it they'll clean up my mess. The media needs a new story. *Sharks attack hapless beachgoers. Another café in the Middle East blown to pieces. Trump's new apprentice designs an L.A. golf course. An insider blows the whistle on the FDA. The FBI hunts down the whistleblower. They need to build another wall.* Tomorrow will have a striking resemblance to today.

Redeemed

The adults must've thought it was cute, me, the only kid present, waving my hand on a Wednesday night, the Music Minister taking requests, asking for Hymn 444. What can I say? My father was pastor. This was my life. I liked the chorus melody, how safe and sure I felt as we sang, piano hammering the heavy accents, simple lyrics lifting—*Redeemed, how I love to proclaim it*—from the *Baptist Hymnal*, carrying out the open side-exit door, where the incandescent glow of headlights and taillights streaming up and down the rocky hillside, were harbingers of God's glory. *Redeemed by the blood of the Lamb.* When turned heavenward, my father's index finger stood for Sermon Point Number 1. The bare hand slapping the pulpit was God making a point, righteous anger, like flooding the world to save it. *Redeemed, how I love to proclaim it.* The finger, the open palm, flesh against flesh, the means to transcending flesh. What does a child know of redemption? These were my most faithful moments—juice was blood. The pulpit, an arc on which I was crossing the bay, which wasn't a bay but a baptistery. *Redeemed by the blood of the Lamb.* The world's literal imagination lifting itself from the shadows. The spires of the distant bridge were steeples, and boats with sails, doves wings, and then they become my father's robe, bathed in white, fluttering around me as he lay me back. When I rise he says, "This is my son in whom I am pleased. Come, all who are weary and heavy-laden. Rise and sin no more."

Following My Calling

I followed my calling out the door. I was upset, my calling has a mind of its own, speaks in all manner of strange tongues. I studied Greek to conjugate my calling's verbs. I transliterated Hebrew trying to get to the bottom of these word pictures. Even after years of español, still I'm at a loss. I realize my calling's very name implies I'm the one who needs to listen, so why all the mystery? A calling follows its heart, right? Should I just tag along like I don't have my own friends? What's the big idea? Would it rather me follow the Tao to a den of silence? All I hear is nothing when it's silent. Am I supposed to hear my calling in some still small voice from a flame in the middle of God knows where? It's got to go around slamming doors like some petulant adolescent? Am I supposed to command it home? My calling couldn't find home if it knocked itself in the solar plexus. The time I had to track it to the Swiss Alps at the End of the World, I knew I'd seen it all. Yodeling from the top of Mount Titleis. I was out of breath by the time I hiked all the way up, and it just stood there not even acknowledging my presence. "Look," I said, "everyone fights. Let's go back to being friends." But my calling just went on yelling its name, letting it echo against the next mountain and the next. "Let's go back," I said. It looked at me like I just don't get it, but you know what? Some of us have jobs. If it wants to sit around all morning flitting around in mystic bliss let it. All I know is my calling wants it both ways. What good is it in saying anything?

Tantrum

And now I am the father—impatient, impenitent, the tension of a thousand disobedient days squeezing the five fists of my heart, some disembodied voice knotting in my throat. *Stop it*, I say. *Clean it up. Last chance.* A thousand days of practiced patience, perhaps, lost to this moment's memory—snapping the plastic robot's head, kicking Hot Wheels cars, flinging Mr. Potato Head pieces at the wall, stomping stuffed animals, the bookcase and TV stand crashing to the floor. *Let this be a lesson*, I say. Only to find the house dark, the driveway empty. I bend over, start picking up the broken pieces.

No Home

When I wandered the earth pining for a divine call, I wondered daily what the dead know. I was a minister in training. I held the hand of a man who was about to find out, sang hymns with the Shut Ins, listened to the mother whose daughter had to be corkscrewed from her car with the Jaws of Life. *Tell me*, they said. They wanted me set apart, wanted to believe in my belief. So I would say, *We have no home in this world*. This is what they wanted, every last one.

Dear Just Visiting this Planet,

Just think of the suffering of all the nameless it took to bring you here. Your whole head is a universe. Your birth canal splits a continent in two. You speak in a language of lava lamps and eight-ball fortunes. Your wardrobe is pure hemp. You're not sinking back into your old habit of dining in the holes of fallen stars are you? Did you know at the speed of light you can arrive at GS-3150 in less than 20 years? Wherever you go there you are. How many more flame outs? I'm a planetarium for your soul. Tomorrow is a satellite.

Signs as Clues and Sometimes Wonders

Flies scattered like startled birds from Matador, my black lab who'd been lost for days. He'd cleared the wall at Lover's Leap, plunged 100 feet to the Brazos' banks. A whippoorwill split the river's middle when I explained all this to a girl I was convinced should believe in the spiritual world. This morning a twister ripped through the valley. Where a house had been standing only splintered pine, loose bricks, Miller High Life can, yesterday's headline. Next door the roof opened to the sky. The wind might've swept my wife and me from our dreams, crushed us into a deeper sleep, but it didn't. They say nothing like this had ever happened before.

If You Want to Be Famous

you can be beautiful or you can live longer than Jeanne Louis Calment from Southern France who lived 122 years, 164 days. Every day thousands of names die. Every day thousands of nameless are born, but no one so far has ever been born to grow as short as Gul Mohammed's 22.5 inches. At any given moment of every day someone hiccups, but who will hiccup longer than Charles Osborn? Through 68 years and two wives he hiccupped some 40 times a minute, and a year after the hiccups went away, so did he. My psychiatrist tells me about some poet I've never heard of who wrote at least one sonnet a day until he reached 10,000. "Of course," he says, "he had Hypo-Manic Disorder." Every day someone fills their mouth with cigarettes, but no one has ever jammed in more than 120, the record now going on 20 years by I forget who. Every day a woman needles another tattoo onto her skin until every orifice is filled in black. Then, all over again in white. Layer after layer. Every day like this. Every day someone in any given wharftown or barrio injects himself, but who will ever be remembered among them when Benjamin Drucker had 745 18-gauge needles inserted into his body on an ordinary afternoon like this? Who will ever survive a bomb going off in mid-flight, and then fall from 33,330 feet, as Vesha Vulovic, a stewardess, did, breaking only an ankle and leg? Every day is a paradise of stats.

Insomniac

When it's afternoon and I can't shake the limbs of the moon from my eyes, the Southern Freight train rolls down the tracks in my head, splitting the Chickamauga Dam to one side, the Tennessee River to the other. If not the limbs and the moon and the Southern Freight, twilight will have settled in with its stadium lights snapped on, an over-wattage game processing into a mindless dawn of extra innings. That's where I'll be this evening when you see me buying this morning's paper at the corner stand on 7th and Grove, shooting the gap, rounding the bases, tipping my cap to the fans who dig the long ball. If not quite scoring, I'll be on deck, timing my swing with a double-barreled Louisville Slugger. There is the life that lives to one side of the night and one that lives to the other. My neighbor's bumper sticker says *Just visiting this planet*. If not this planet then the next orbit, maybe a constellation of galactic troposphere's the exact right distance from some red sun in a part of the universe as yet undeveloped. If not some new physical realm of the ever-expanding universe, then its reverse negative, a peering into the multi-linear platitudes of the Hubble telescope's billion dollar past, that mythological time construct where everything flings itself as reckless as dreamless vagrants, wandering shadows in search of some Technicolor world. If not mind-boggling speeds and time warps, just a snapshot or two down the road, just Bugs Bunny pulling the curtain on my tombstone, *That's all folks*, and a bunch of credits rolling anonymous names.

Notes

"The Meaning of Chad"—Chad also means *warrior* but Chad would rather fight for peace.

"Seven Lightning Strikes"—Roy C. Sullivan (1912-1983) is the world record holder as the man struck seven times by lightning. There is a road side plaque in Tanner's Ridge in Page County, VA that talks about Roy. This poem is inspired from his record but is otherwise a work of fiction.

The last line of "Letter to Zarathustra from Hypochondriac" comes from a line from Canio (as quoted from Richard Jackson): "Laugh at the sorrow that destroys your heart."

"Letter to a Suicide Letter"—The last line is taken from Thomas Lux's "Elegy for Frank Stanford" (*Sunday*). Jeremy's real name has been changed for artistic purposes and to protect the innocent.

"Notes Toward What Volcanologists Know"—published first as a prose poem by *Redactions*. Also published as a lineated poem by Word Tech Press (*Snapshots of the Perishing World*).

"Bowing Not Knowing to What" borrows its phrase from W.S. Merwin's "Lines for the Anniversary of My Death."

"Chad Prevost Chases Chad Prevost"—Originally inspired by Gerry LaFemina's "On Seeing the Ghost of My Adolescence" (*23 Below*). For years I tinkered with the poem, then one day I came across Christopher Buckley's anthology *Homage to Vallejo* and was inspired to incorporate a sub-text into the narrative dealing with predicting one's own death as related to Vallejo's famous "White Stone Sitting on a Black Stone." I felt this gave the poem an essential textual layering. "Poetry from poetry," as Buckley's introduction asserts.

"Dear Light Those at Work See" borrows its title from George Kalamaras' "The Light Those at Work See" from *Even the Java Sparrows Call Your Hair*

(Quale Press). The inspiration for interspersing a more direct epistolary form of address with all the "Dear" titles also comes from Kalamaras' work.

Poems with significantly changed or altered titles: "Where the Light is Still Good" published as "Stepping Inside, Mount Tamalpais"; "Rehearsing" published as "Recording Our Time"; "The End of the World" published as "Wanted: Branch Davidian"; "Letter to a Suicide Letter" published as "Looking for a Miracle"; "Muted Blues Bird" published as "Valerie Listening to Old Recordings"; "Chad Prevost Chases Chad Prevost" published as "Chasing the Ghost"; "Baptism by Fire" published as "After Punishment, Baptism."

"Baptism by Fire" is for my parents and inspired by Arthur Smith.

Special Thanks for inspiration, courage, and ideas throughout this book to: George Kalamaras, Gary Young, Gerry LaFemina, Robin Hemley, John Bradley, Mike Dockins, Michael Martone.

About the Author

Chad Prevost was born in Marin General Hospital in Fairfax, California and divided his childhood between there and Chicago, Morgantown, Phoenix, and Richmond. Prevost is the offspring of Mr. Mississippi College 1968 and The Queen of the Forest Beauty Pageant 1967. In other words, genetics alone might have suggested Prevost was destined for success as an all-around personable, high-achieving, handsome young man. His parents both graduated from high school and college with perfect GPAs. During the 70s in California when it was the style to wear one's hair slightly longish, Prevost's father looked a bit like Tom Sellek of *Magnum P.I.* It helped that Prevost's father was also named Tom. Over the years, however, Prevost's father's hair line receded until the center of his father's hair line was but a squiggle resembling a question mark. Nevertheless, with a beauty pageant winner mother and a father that resembled Tom Sellek other than a receding hair line, Prevost felt certain he would grow from a cute kid into a handsome man. In fact, as Prevost grew tall and lean and his blond hair lightened in the summer sun, someone mentioned that he resembled Val Kilmer, who played Ice Man in *Top Gun*. He was also told that he looked like Ricky Shroeder from *Silver Spoons*, and also the brother of Robb Lowe, Chad Lowe, who starred in his own sit-com for a brief stint, *Spencer*. Prevost especially liked the idea that he looked like Chad Lowe since they shared the same first name. These glory days, however, were all only a mere brief stint on the radar of Prevost's life just before puberty arrived. Before he knew it, Prevost far more resembled Goose, played by Anthony Edwards than Val Kilmer. Prevost had yet to come to terms with a feature he inherited from his father, a feature he had overlooked in his father and a feature that really kept his father from resembling Tom Sellek beyond the mere receding hairline. That feature was a weak chin. Prevost inherited his father's jaw line which is barely a line at all. Prevost had the misfortune of inheriting his mother's long neck and missing out on her strong chin. Whereas a long neck is graceful on a woman, it tends to produce chicken-like necks in men whose Adams Apple sticks out almost like a second nose. Prevost was also slow in developing the substantial facial hair of his father. One of Prevost's issues related to the shade of the hair itself. Whereas the hair on his chin was a dark brown, the hair on his upper lip was a light blond, virtually undetectable unless one got up very close. When he was 21 and serving as a Youth Minister at Williams Trace Baptist Church in Sugar Land, Texas, Prevost had had enough of his moustache's fairness, and decided to darken it. By darkening the blond hairs, Prevost believed he would finally achieve that Tom Sellek-like handsomeness, possibly appearing more generally distinguished and even perhaps a bit biblical. Two treatments of the Just for Men dye didn't do much, so Prevost treated it again and again until he believed it evenly matched the color of his eyebrows. Prevost actually went around like this with an almost black moustache at the age of 21 for a week before he had second thoughts and just shaved the whole thing off. As Prevost grew older and finally did put on a little weight, his neck merged with his chin. Occasionally, a student would try to ingratiate herself with Prevost by noting that Prevost did seem to have an uncanny resemblance to Owen Wilson. Prevost liked Wilson and believed him to be as cool as the characters he played on the silver screen, but did think privately that he had a better nose than Wilson's crooked one. Someone else had noted that Prevost resembled Owen's older brother, Luke Wilson, who had darker hair and although Prevost didn't initially see it, still wanting to believe his brownish hair was blond, Prevost came to believe he did resemble the elder Wilson. After decades of denial about just how weak his chin was, Prevost finally decided that the best way to overcome the physical deficiency was to grow a goatee which would give his chin more substance and hide the merging line between his chin and neck. This backfired on Prevost as he came to resemble the skinny, chinless, hairline-receding, Canadian comic Tom Green. To this day, whenever Prevost dares to grow any facial hair, people stop him on the streets, in hallways, at bars and ask Prevost if he, Tom Green, will sign their autograph, and they won't take no for an answer.

Chad will neither confirm nor deny whether or not he is the aging rock star, the walking cliché or any of the other random and assorted characters and speakers parading through this book, even the ones bearing his name.